DEVELOPING OBJECT ORIENTED PROGRAMS IN JAVA

THEORY & PRACTICE ON OOP AS PER ANNA UNIVERSITY SYLLABUS

DAVID LIVINGSTON J

ISBN 979-888530752-9

This book has been dedicated to God Almighty and His Son Jesus Christ, who gives Knowledge and Wisdom abundantly to those who call on His Name.

The Proverbs 1:7 written by King Solomon, a King renwned for his Knowledge through out the world, says like this:

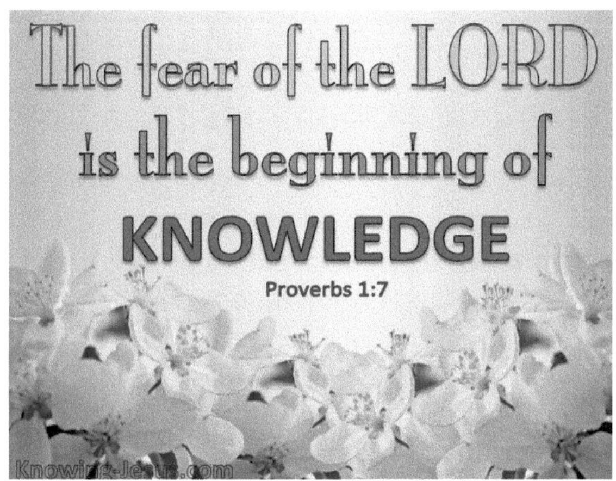

Proverbs 1:7

Contents

PREFACE

This book titled "Object Oriented Programming" having the subject code CS8392 has been written for the students of Computer Science and Engineering doing their studies in Engineering Colleges affiliated to Anna University, Chennai.

This book has covered the topics related to Object Oriented Programming as per the syllabus framed by Anna University. Following are the major topics covered in Five Units framed by the University for learning Object Oriented Programming using JAVA:

1. Introduction to Object Oriented Programming and JAVA
2. Implementing Inheritance and Interfaces in JAVA
3. Handling Exceptions and Input Output operations in JAVA
4. Multithreading and Generic Programming in JAVA
5. Event Driven Programming using AWS in JAVA

SECTION I - Introducing Object Oriented Programming & JAVA

Topics Covered in SECTION I:

Introduction to Object Oriented Programming

- Merits and Demerits of Object Oriented Programming
- Object Oriented Concepts
- Frequently Asked Questions on OOP

Introduction to Java - An Object Oriented Language

- Overview of Java
- Basic Structure of a Java Program
- Fundamental Programming Elements in Java

Data Types and Operators in Java

- Primitive Datatypes in Java
- Operators in Java

I

Introduction to Object Oriented Programming

In Object Oriented model of programming, programs are organized as objects that consist of data and a set of well-defined interfaces (code) that operates on data. And hence, object oriented programs can be characterized as code controlling access to data. Object oriented languages combine both data and functions, the core elements of a program into a single entity called object. Objects allow localization of data and code and restrict other objects from referring to their local region.

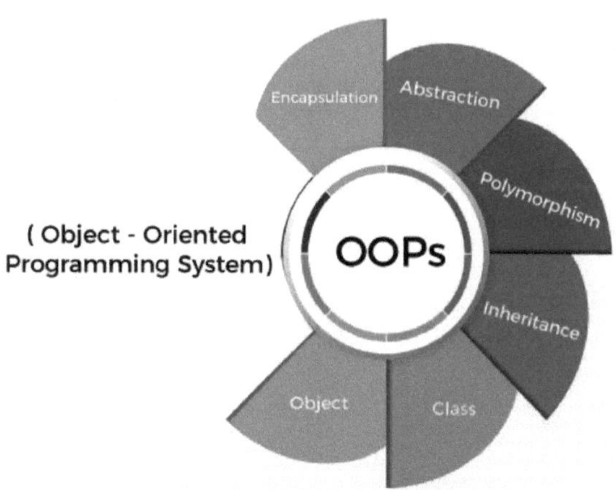

Fig. 1.1 - Fundamental Concepts of Object Oriented Programming

Object Oriented Programming (OOP) treats data as the critical element in a program and does not allow the data to flow freely around the system. It ties the data more closely to the functions that operate on them and protects them from accidental modifications from other parts of the program.

he protected data can be freely accessed only from the functions that are associated with them. However, the functions of one object can access the functions of another object. The following are some of the striking features of OOP:

1. Emphasis is on data rather than procedure.
2. Programs are divided into what are known as objects.
3. Date and functions that operate on data are tied together into an entity called object.
4. Data are hidden within the object and can't be directly accessed by external functions.
5. New data and functions can be easily added whenever necessary and
6. Follows bottom-up approach in program design.

The organization of data and functions in object-oriented programs is shown in the above figure. Consider an object - account with three attributes: AccountNumber, AccountType, Name and Balance, and three operations: Deposit, Withdraw, and Enquire. The pictorial notation of this object is shown in the below figure:

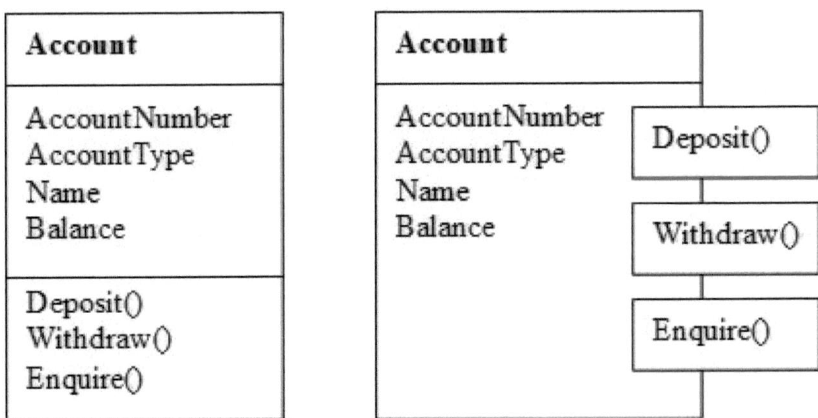

Fig. 1.2 - Two Different Representation of Account Object

The main advantage of using OO approach is reusability. Through this mechanism, an object already written can be reused to minimize the time and effort required to rewrite similar kind of objects. When a new object requires similar set of functionalities of an existing object and some additional features, instead of designing it from scratch, we can derive (create) it from an existing one.

Merits and Demerits of Object Oriented Programming

Object-oriented design involves identification and implementation of different classes of objects and their behavior in a real world problem. The objects in a software system closely correspond and relate to the objects in the real world in a one-to-one manner. Thus, it is easier to design and implement a system consisting of objects.

OOP languages provide a programmer the ability to create modular and reusable code using which formulating a new program can be done easily by composition and modification of some existing modules. The co-operation among different objects is achieved through exchange of messages.

Merits:

Since the objects are autonomous entities and share their responsibilities only by executing methods relevant to the received messages, each object lends itself to greater modularity. Flexibility is also gained by being able to change or replace modules without disturbing other parts of the code. Moreover, the independence of each object eases development and maintenance of the program.

The following are some of the merits of Object Oriented methodology:

- Information hiding and data abstraction increase reliability and help decouple the procedural and representational specification from its implementation.
- Dynamic binding increases flexibility by permitting the addition of new classes of objects without having to modify the existing code.
- Inheritance coupled with dynamic binding enhances the reusability of code, thus increasing the productivity of a programmer.
- Many OO languages provide a standard class library that can be extended (extend ability) by the users, thus saving a lot of coding and debugging effort.
- The advantages of object orientation also includes: shorter development time, high degree of code sharing and malleability (can be molded to any shape).

Demerits:

The runtime cost of dynamic binding mechanism is the major disadvantage of object-oriented languages. The following were the demerits of adopting object-orientation in software development in the early days of computing (some remain forever):

- Compile time and Run time overhead
- Re-orientation of software developer to object-orientated thinking
- Requires the master over the following areas:
    - Software Engineering
    - Programming Methodologies
    - Benefits only in long run while managing large software projects, at least moderately large ones.

Object Oriented Concepts

Object-oriented programming is a powerful and natural paradigm for creating programs that survive the inevitable changes accompanying the life cycle of any major software projects including conception, grown and aging.

An object is an entity in a real-world problem. It may represent a person, a place, a bank account, a table of data or any other item in the real world. In software scenario, an object refers to a piece of software containing data and code that can be reused.

An object in a running program takes up space in memory and has an associated address to refer to it. Examples for objects used in a banking application are: “customer” and “account.” During execution, objects interact with each other by sending messages and receiving responses.

Class & Object:

Class is a user-defined data type, which defines the structure of an object. Objects are variables or instances of type class. A class defines the type and scope of all its members.

There are two elements defined in a class. They are variables and functions. Variables declared in a class are called data members, and the functions defined in a class are known as member functions.

Every class describes possibly infinite set of individual objects; each object is said to be an instance of its class and each instance has its own value for each attribute. Following are the various definitions of ‘class’ data type:

1. A class is a template that unites data and operations.
2. A class is an abstraction of real world entities having similar properties.
3. A class identifies a set of similar objects.

Abstraction:

Abstraction refers to the act of representing essential features of an object without exposing the internal implementations of it. A sequence of code (processing steps) can be abstracted by putting them into a function (called interface) and allowing the user to access the function by knowing its function signature (function name, parameters and the return type) without knowing the code used for implementing the function.

Each and every method or variable defined in a class may be marked as private or public. The public members of a class represent everything the external users of the class need to know about. The private methods or data can only be accessed by methods that is a member of the class.

In an object-oriented program, objects contain both data and functions (methods) that operate on data. The data are not accessible directly from the outside world, but only the methods. This act of insulating or hiding data from public access from outside the object is called data abstraction or data hiding.

The arrangement of data from a process-oriented model can be transformed by abstracting the data into a component called object in object-oriented model. Only the functions of the object can access the data hidden in an object freely.

Encapsulation:

In an object-oriented language like Java, the basis of encapsulation is the class. In a class, we define both variables and functions that operate on the variables defined in it. Collectively these elements – data and functions are called members of a class. The variables defined in a class are known as member variables or instance variables. The functions that operate on the variables of a class are referred to as member functions or methods.

The wrapping up of data and functions into a single unit (called class) is known as encapsulation. Encapsulation binds data and the code that operates on data and keeps both of them safe from outside interference and misuse. Though a class contains both data and functions, only the functions are available to the public, but not the data. The encapsulated data within the class are not accessible from outside world directly.

The hidden data can be accessed only through the member functions, which act as interfaces between the data and the external program. By declaring variables as private members, we can hide the data of an object. Variables declared as protected also implement data hiding. Such an act of hiding the data from public access is also referred to as data abstraction.

Polymorphism:

Polymorphism means having one name but different forms. Polymorphism allows two member functions of a same class to have the same name, but different parameters or return type. There are two types of polymorphism: Compile-time polymorphism and Run-time polymorphism.

Function overloading is an example for compile-time polymorphism. Two functions are said to be overloaded when they have the same name but different number/type of parameters or return type. Since the selection of an overloaded function is determined at compile time by the compiler based on the parameter passed during function call, this type of polymorphism is called compile-time polymorphism.

Run-time polymorphism occurs during the function call of an over-ridden function. When a function of a base class (a class used for defining another class) is redefined in its derived class (class newly created from an existing one), it can have the same name, the same set of parameters and the return type as that of the base class function, but different body (i.e., with different implementation). In such a case, the selection of the function (function of the base class or the derived class) to be executed will be determined at run-time by the compiler. Hence, function overriding is an example for run-time polymorphism.

Inheritance:

If we want to model an object whose functionality is basically similar to that of another object, then the new object can derive its basic functionalities from an already existing object. For example, the object 'plastic chair' inherits all the basic qualities like arms, legs and seat from an idol chair in addition to the extra qualification "material used" for making it.

Inheritance is a concept of OOP that defines the mechanism for creating a new class from an existing class called base class. The base class can be added on or altered to create the new class called derived class. In this way, a hierarchy of related classes can be created and reused in an object oriented programming.

Frequently Asked Questions (FAQ)

1. How is OOP different from procedural oriented programming?

Structured programming and OOP fundamentally differ in one issue: the way they view the core elements of the program – data and functions. Structured programming views data and functions as two separate entities, whereas OOP views them as a single entity.

2. What do you mean by Top-down design?

In structured programming method, we use the Top-Down approach, in which the overall objective of the system is defined first. Then the system is divided into various sub tasks or sub modules. In this methodology, software development is done by writing a group of sub programs, and then collecting or integrating them together to form a complex system.

3. Name some of the fundamental features of OOP?

OOP is designed around the data being operated upon as opposed to the operations themselves. The power of object-oriented languages is that the programmer can create modular, reusable code and as a result, formulate a program by composing and modifying the existing models. The fundamental features of OOP are the following:

- Encapsulation
- Data Abstraction
- Inheritance
- Polymorphism and
- Extensibility

4. Name at least two OOPs languages other than Java.

C++ and Smalltalk are the two object oriented languages that support important feature of OOP languages such as polymorphism, inheritance, and message based communication.

5. What are the benefits of Object Oriented Programming?

The following are the major benefits of OOP:

- Modeling the real-world problem as close as possible to the user's perspective.
- Interacting easily with computational environment using familiar metaphors.
- Constructing reusable software components and easily extendable libraries.
- Easily modifying and extending implementations of components without having to recode everything from scratch.

6. What are User-defined Data types? Give examples.

User-defined data type is a data type defined by the user himself. The user can define his/her own data type using the data types already given in the language. Examples for built-in or primary data types are: int, float, char, and double. Some of the examples for the user-defined data types are: Class, Structure and Enumerator.

7. Distinguish between Class and Object.

A Class is a user-defined data type, which defines the structure of an object. It defines the type and scope of all its members, where as, objects are variables or instances of type class.

An object is an entity in the real-world problem. It may represent a person, a place, a bank account, a table of data or any other item in the real world.

8. What do you mean by Data Hiding?

Data hiding is nothing but hiding or abstracting the private data of an object from the direct access of other parts of the program. Though a class contains both data and functions that operate on the data, only the public functions are available for access, but not the private data.

9. Define Abstraction and Encapsulation. How are these terms interrelated?

The wrapping up of data and functions into a single unit (called class) is known as Encapsulation. But the word 'Abstraction' refers to the act of hiding something.

Hiding the private data from public access of other parts of the program is known as Data Abstraction. By declaring the variables as private, we can hide the data of an object. Variables declared as protected also implement data hiding.

II

Introduction to JAVA - An Object Oriented Language

In 1990, Sun Microsystems decided to develop special software that could be used to manipulate consumer electronic devices. A team of Sun Microsystems programmers headed by James Gosling was formed to undertake this task. After exploring the possibility of using popular Object Oriented languages such as Smalltalk and C++, the team announced a new language named Oak in 1991. Oak was lter renamed to Java.

Fig. 2.1 - Various Programming Languages for Application Development

Java has the following features (characteristics) most of which are not to be found in other Object Oriented languages such as C++ and Smalltalk:

i. **Java is simple to learn and use**: Programmers of Java found it easy to write and debug java programs.
ii. **Secured**: Java programs are confined to run in a container called Java Runtime Environment (JRE). And hence they can't access resources like memory outside the runtime environment.
iii. **Purely Object Oriented**: Java programs require the use of classes and objects to write even a simple program like displaying "Hello, World!" in an object oriented way.
iv. **Portable**: Java is a platform independent language. Because, java programs are converted into byte code first, and then the byte code is interpreted by Java Runtime System called Java Virtual Machine (JVM). Hence, java programs can be executed anywhere and on any system without recompiling the same program compiled once.
v. **Multi-threaded**: Java supports multi-threading. Using Java, we can write a program that can run multiple taks simultaneously.
vi. **Java is scalable**: Java programs can run not only on Desktop/Laptop computers, they can also be written to run on any electronic appliances such as washing machine.

The Java Environment

The Java Development Kit (JDK) is actually a combination of Java compilation tools and API implementation for a particular version of the Java Platform. It also typically includes a Java runtime (JRE), so that you can run the programs you compile. JDK comprises the following development tools:

- **java**: Serves as a Java interpreter used to run Java applets and applications by reading and interpreting bytecode files
- **javac**: Serves as a Java compiler used to translate Java source code files.
- **javadoc**: Creates HTML documentation for Java source code files
- **javap:** Serves as a Java disassemble used to convert bytecode files into a Java program description
- **jdb:** Serves as a Java debugger used to find errors in Java programs
- **appletviewer**: Facilitates to run Java applets
- **jar**: Serves as archive used to package related class libraries into a single executable JAR file. This tool also helps to manage the JAR files
- **javah**: Serves as the C header and stub generator, which is used to write native methods.

Overview of Java

Java is a general purpose, Object Oriented language. With the help of Java, a programmer can develop different kinds of applications that include:

a. Standalone applications
b. Internet applications
c. Mobile applications

Standalone Applications:

Standalone applications are programs written in a higher level language like Java to carry out certain tasks on a standalong local computer. Standalong application runs on a single computer and it does not require any network connection for its execution.

Executing a standalong Java program involves two steps:

1. Compile the source code into byte code using **javac** compiler, a part of JDK.
2. Execute the byte code form of the program using **java** interpreter, another tool in JDK.

Internet Applicatons:

Applets are small java programs developed for Internet applications. Using applets, onecan develop animated graphics as well as games that can run on the Internet. An applet located on a remote computer (server machine) can be downloaded via Internet and get executed on a local computer (client machine) using a web browser.

An applet can run only using a web browser like Internet Explorer or Chrome. JDK also provides a tool named **appletviewer**, using which applets can run on a standalone computer. HotJava, a browser developed for running applets, is also developed using Java language.

Mobile Applications:

Java is the language of choice for developing mobile applications that can run on handheld devices like mobile phones. Such a development of mobile applications for hand held devices are also known as android application development.

Android is an open source software platform and Linux-based operating system for mobile devices. The Android platform allows developers to write managed code using Java to manage and control the Android device. Android applications can be developed by using the Java programming language and the Android SDK. So, familiarity with the basics of the Java programming language is a prerequisite for programming on the Android platform.

Basic Structure of a Java Program

Java is an Object Oriented programming language, which follows OO concepts strictly for the development of its program. In Java, even a simple program like the one that display the message "Hello, World!" would require a class, an object-oriented element. Every program in Java starts with the word 'class'.

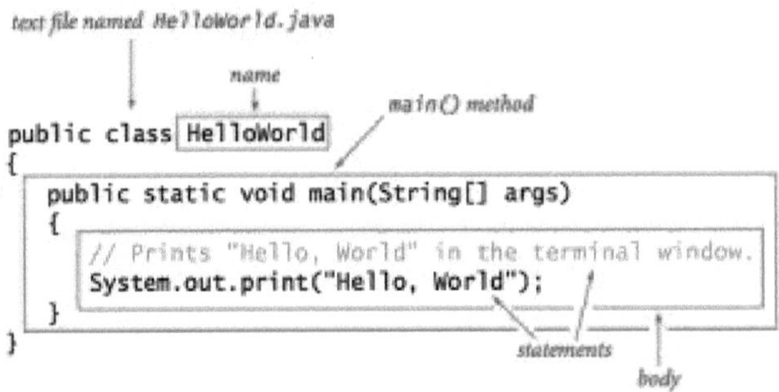

Fig. 2.2 - Basic Structure of a Java Program

Without using the basic OO concepts (Class and Object), it is not possible to write a program in Java. The following is a simple "Hello, World!" program in Java:

```
class Example{
public static void main(String args[]){
System.out.println("Hello, World!");
}}
```

In this Java program, *Example* is the name of the program, and is defined as a class. While running this program through Java runtime system, an instance of the class *Example* is created and is called an **Application Object**. Hence, a Java program itself is an object, which will use other objects in it.

Method main() in Java:

As in the class *Example*, every java program will have a public member function named *main( )*. This function is the starting point for every Java program. As soon as an application is created, the function *main( )* will be called by the OS to run the program. This function must be declared as *public* for start up.

The function *main( )* has got one parameter, which is an array of strings. Through this parameter, user input can be passed to *main( )* from command-line at the time of starting the application. As the dimension of this array is not specified, any no. of strings (messages) can be passed as input to the application.

In the above example, there is only one statement written in function *main( )* for displaying the message "*Hello, World!*". It is an output statement with two objects: ***system*** and ***out***. The first object '*system*' refers to the computer and the second object '*out*' refers to an output device to which the message has to be sent for display. The object '*out*' provides an operation called ***println***, using which the output can be displayed in the output device.

Fundamental Programming Elements of Java

Smallest individual element is known as token. The tokens in java are are classified as: Keywords, Identifiers, Literals, Constants, Separators and Operators. Keywords are special words defined in Java for a special purpose. They are not to be used as naming words for any element of a program. Here is a list of keywords in Java:

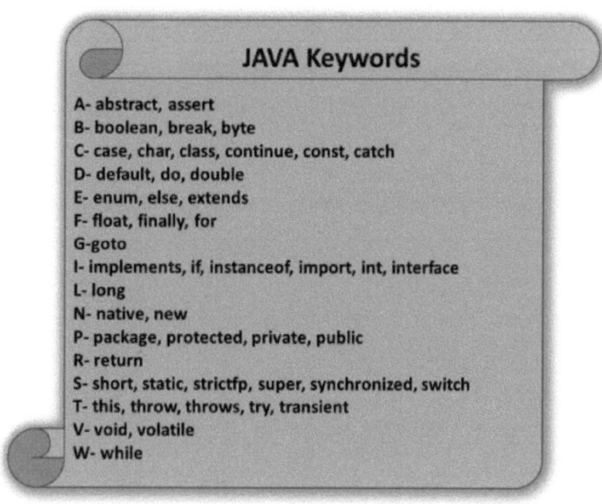

Fig. 2.3 - Keywords Provided in Java

Identifiers

- An identifier is a name given to a variable, method, class, package, or an interface in Java
- Java identifiers consist of alphabets, numbers, underscore(_), and the dollar sign ($)

Legal Indentifers

- Identifiers must start with a letter, a currency character ($), or a connecting character such as the underscore (_). Identifiers cannot start with a number!
- After the first character, identifiers can contain any combination of letters, currency characters, connecting characters, or numbers. Does not allow spaces in between an identifier.
- In practice, there is no limit to the number of characters an identifier can contain.
- We can't use a Java keyword as an identifier.
- Identifiers in Java are case-sensitive; so pen and PEN are two different identifiers.

Literals

- Literal denotes any value assigned to a variable used in a program. Based on the datatype, literals stored or defined in a program can be of any one of the following types:
  - String Literals
  - Character Literals
  - Boolean Literals
  - Floating Point Literals
  - Integer Literals

Examples:
24 // an int literal
124.543 // a double literal
true // boolean literal
'v' // a char literal

"hello" // a string literal

Escape sequences for String literals

A character preceded by a backslash (\) is an escape sequence and has special meaning to the compiler. The following table shows the Java escape sequences:

Escape SequenceDescription

\t Insert a tab in the text at this point.

\b Insert a backspace in the text at this point.

\n Insert a newline in the text at this point.

\r Insert a carriage return in the text at this point.

\f Insert a formfeed in the text at this point.

\' Insert a single quote character in the text at this point.

\" Insert a double quote character in the text at this point.

\\ Insert a backslash character in the text at this point.

When an escape sequence is encountered in a print statement, the compiler interprets it accordingly. For example, if you want to put quotes within quotes you must use the escape sequence, \", on the interior quotes. To print the sentence:

She said "Hello!" to me.

you would write

System.out.println("She said \"Hello!\" to me.");

Separators

Separators are symbols or special characters used to separate one part of the program from another. Some of them are as follows:

- Parentheses ( )
- Braces [ ]
- Brackets { }
- Semicolon ;
- Colon :
- Period .
- Comma ,

Separators help us defining the structure of a program. The most commonly used separator in java is a semicolon(;). Because every line of statement in Java ends with a semicolon.

Operators

An operator is a symbol that implies some special meaning in a program. For instance, an arithmetic operator like +, -. *, / or % allows a programmer to form an arithmetic expression a set of constants and variables.

III

Data Types and Operators in Java

Variables are nothing but reserved memory locations to store values. This means that when you declare a variable we reserve some space in memory. Based on the data type of a variable, the operating system allocates memory and decides what can be stored in the reserved memory. Therefore, by assigning different data types to variables, we can store data of type integers, decimals, or characters in these variables.

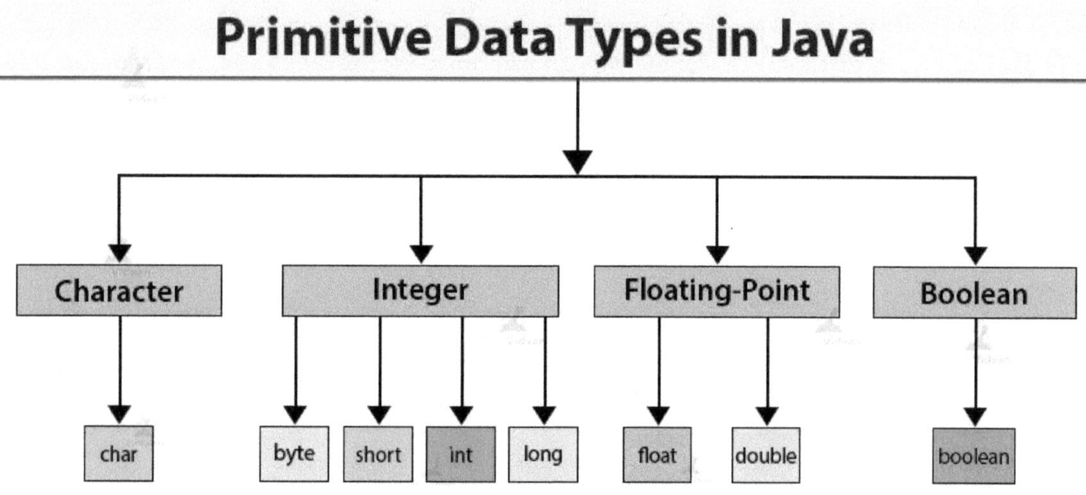

Fig 3.1 - Fundamental Data Types of Java

Java is a strongly type language. It is more strictly typed than any other OOP language. This fact is justified based on the following three facts:

1. Every variable and expression used in Java has a type. And every type is strongly defined.
2. All assignments, whether explicit or via parameter passing in method calls are checked for type compatibility.
3. Java doesn't support automatic coercion or conversions of conflicting types. All expressions and parameters are checked by Java compiler for type compatibility.

There are two types of data types in Java:
Primitive datatypes - Integer, Floating, Charachter, Boolean.
Referential datatypes - Arrays, Class objects
Java defines eight simple (or primitive) data types: byte, short, int, long, char, float, double and boolean. These can be put in four groups:

i. **Integer** data types – which include byte, short, int and long
ii. **Floating-point** numbers – float and double
iii. **Character** and
iv. **Boolean**

The simple data types represent single values. We can use them for declaring ordinary variables, constructing arrays, or user-defined data types like class. Because of Java's portability requirement, all data types have a strictly defined range. For instance, an **int** always occupies 32 bits, regardless of the particular platform. This allows programs to be written on one platform and then ported to another platform for execution without any modification of its source code.

Integer Data Types

Integer data types are used to store integer data items. **Java supports only the signed integers,** therefore the integer types have both +ve and -ve values. Java provides four integer data types to store the integer values.
The variables can be declared in the following ways:
byte x;
short sum;
int age;
long milliseconds; //The long data type can be also declared by appending l or L at the end of the data. For example 125L denotes long datatype.

Floating Data Types:

Floating-point numbers, also known as real numbers, are used when evaluating expressions that require fractional precision. The type **float** specifies a single-precision value that uses 32 bits of storage. Single precision is faster on some processors and takes half as much space as double precision, but will become imprecise when the values are either very large or very small.

A float datatype can store maximum 7 digits after the decimal point. While delcaring and using float data type, we must add the character f or F as postfix to the data. Without the postfix, a compilation error will occur as all floating point numbers are considered as double in Java.

float height = 6.1; //incorrect

float height = 6.1f; //correct

Double precision, as denoted by the **double** keyword, uses 64 bits to store a value.

double pi = 3.14; //correct

double pi = 3.14d; //correct

Character Data Type:

The charachter data type is used to represent and store the charachter constants in Java programs. The character data type availaible in Java is char. This data type follows the Unicode charachter set.

The char data type has a width of **2 bytes**. The range of a char is **0 to 65,536**

char grade = 'A';

Boolean Datatypes:

The boolean data type represents two logical values denoted by true or false. This is the type returned by all relational operators such as a<b.

boolean x = true;

Reference Data Types:

Reference variables are created using defined constructors of the classes. They are used to access objects. These variables are declared to be of a specific type that cannot be changed. For example, Employee, Puppy etc.

Class objects, and various type of array variables come under reference data type. Default value of any reference variable is null. A reference variable can be used to refer to any object of the declared type or any compatible type.

Example :

Animal animal = new Animal("giraffe");

Wrapper Classes:

Java provides six primitive data types for data storage, namely, int, float, long, char and double. Apart from these, it also provides wrapper classes for the conversion of primitive data types into object data types. Such classes are available in the package java.lang. Using these classes, we can store and manipulate the data in objects. The following are the data types and their corresponding wrapper classes in Java:

boolean Boolean

char Character

double Double

float Float

int Integer

long Long

Operators in Java

Learning the operators of the Java programming language is a good place to start. Operators are special symbols that perform specific operations on one, two, or three operands, and then return a result. This section explains various operators supported by the Java programming language.

Simple Assignment Operator

= Simple assignment operator

Arithmetic Operators

Java programming language provides operators that perform addition, subtraction, multiplication, and division. They are listed below:

+ Additive operator (also used for String concatenation)

- Subtraction operator

* Multiplication operator

/ Division operator

% Remainder operator

The following program, ArithmeticDemo, demonstrates the use of arithmetic operators.

“*class ArithmeticDemo {*

```
public static void main (String[] args) {
int result = 1 + 2; // result is now 3
System.out.println("1 + 2 = " + result);
int original_result = result;
result = result - 1; // result is now 2
System.out.println(original_result + " - 1 = " + result);
original_result = result;
result = result * 2; // result is now 4
System.out.println(original_result + " * 2 = " + result);
original_result = result; result = result / 2; // result is now 2
System.out.println(original_result + " / 2 = " + result);
original_result = result; result = result + 8; // result is now 10
System.out.println(original_result + " + 8 = " + result);
original_result = result; result = result % 7; // result is now 3
System.out.println(original_result + " % 7 = " + result);
}}"
```

This program prints the following:

```
1 + 2 = 3
3 - 1 = 2
2 * 2 = 4
4 / 2 = 2
2 + 8 = 10
10 % 7 = 3
```

You can also combine the arithmetic operators with the simple assignment operator to create compound assignments. For example, x+=1; and x=x+1; both increment the value of x by 1.

The + operator can also be used for concatenating (joining) two strings together, as shown in the following ConcatDemo program:

```
"class ConcatDemo {
public static void main(String[] args){
String firstString = "This is";
String secondString = " a concatenated string.";
String thirdString = firstString+secondString;
System.out.println(thirdString);
```

```
}}"
```

By the end of this program, the variable thirdString contains "This is a concatenated string.", which gets printed to standard output.

Unary Operators:

+ Unary plus operator; indicates positive value (numbers are positive without this, however)
- Unary minus operator; negates an expression
++ Increment operator; increments a value by 1
-- Decrement operator; decrements a value by 1
! Logical complement operator; inverts the value of a boolean

The following program, UnaryDemo, demonstrate the use of unary operators:

```
"class UnaryDemo {
    public static void main(String[] args) {
    int result = +1; // result is now 1
    System.out.println(result);
    result--; // result is now 0
    System.out.println(result);
    result++; // result is now 1
    System.out.println(result);
    result = -result; // result is now -1
    System.out.println(result);
    boolean success = false; // false
    System.out.println(success); // true
    System.out.println(!success);
    }}"
```

The increment/decrement operators can be applied before (prefix) or after (postfix) the operand. The code result++; and ++result; will both end in result being incremented by one. The only difference is that the prefix version (++result) evaluates to the incremented value, whereas the postfix version (result++) evaluates to the original value. If we are just performing a simple increment/decrement, it doesn't really matter which version you choose. But if we use this operator in part of a larger expression, the one that you choose may make a significant difference.

IV

More Operators in Java

The equality and relational operators determine if one operand is greater than, less than, equal to, or not equal to another operand. The majority of these operators will probably look familiar to you as well.

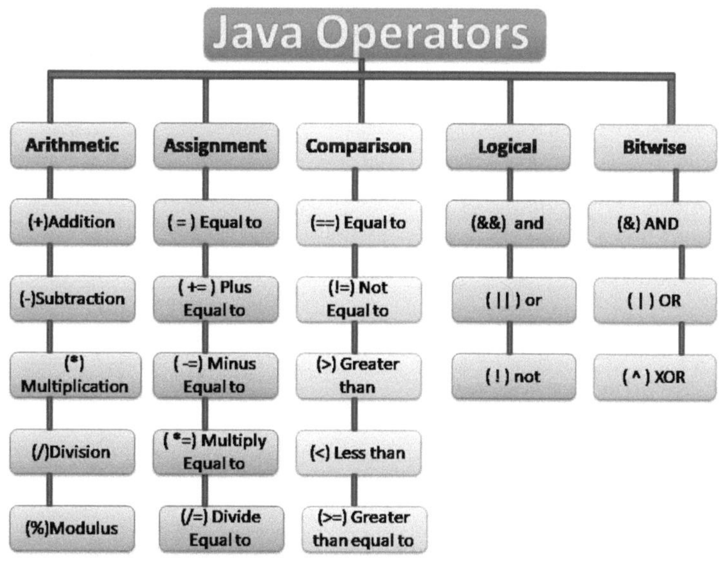

Fig 4.1 List of Operators in Java

Keep in mind that you must use "==", not "=", when testing if two primitive values are equal. The following is the list of relational opertors in Java:

== Equal to

!= Not equal to

> Greater than

>= Greater than or equal to

< Less than

<= Less than or equal to

The following program, ComparisonDemo, demonstrates the use of comparison operators:

```
"class ComparisonDemo {
    public static void main(String[] args){
    int value1 = 1;
    int value2 = 2;
    if(value1 == value2)
    System.out.println("value1 == value2");
    if(value1 != value2)
    System.out.println("value1 != value2");
    if(value1 > value2)
    System.out.println("value1 > value2");
    if(value1 < value2)
    System.out.println("value1 < value2");
    if(value1 <= value2)
    System.out.println("value1 <= value2");
    }}"
```

Output:

```
value1 != value2
value1 < value2
value1 <= value2
```

Logical or Conditional Operators:

The && and || operators perform Conditional-AND and Conditional-OR operations on two boolean expressions. These operators exhibit "short-circuiting" behavior, which means that the second operand is evaluated only if needed.

&& Conditional-AND

|| Conditional-OR

The following program, ConditionalDemo1, illustrates the application of these operators:

```
“class ConditionalDemo1 {
public static void main(String[] args){
int value1 = 1;
int value2 = 2;
if((value1 == 1) && (value2 == 2))
System.out.println("value1 is 1 AND value2 is 2");
if((value1 == 1) || (value2 == 1))
System.out.println("value1 is 1 OR value2 is 1");
}
}”
```

Another conditional operator is ?:, which can be thought of as shorthand for an if-then-else statement (discussed in the Control Flow Statements section of this lesson). This operator is also known as the ternary operator because it uses three operands. In the following example, this operator should be read as: "If someCondition is true, assign the value of value1 to result. Otherwise, assign the value of value2 to result."

The following program, ConditionalDemo2, demonstrates the ?: operator:

```
“class ConditionalDemo2 {
public static void main(String[] args){
int value1 = 1;
int value2 = 2;
int result;
boolean someCondition = true;
result = someCondition ? value1 : value2; System.out.println(result);
}
}”
```

Because someCondition is true, this program prints "1" to the screen. Use the ?: operator instead of an if-then-else statement if it makes your code more readable; for example, when the expressions are compact and without side-effects (such as assignments).

Type Comparison Operator:

The **instanceof** operator compares an object to a specified type. You can use it to test if an object is an instance of a class, an instance of a subclass, or an instance of a class that implements a particular interface.

The following program, InstanceofDemo, defines a parent class (named Parent), a simple interface (named MyInterface), and a child class (named Child) that inherits from the parent and implements the interface.

```
"class InstanceofDemo
{
public static void main(String[] args)
{
Parent obj1 = new Parent();
Parent obj2 = new Child();
System.out.println("obj1 instanceof Parent: " + (obj1 instanceof Parent));
System.out.println("obj1 instanceof Child: " + (obj1 instanceof Child));
System.out.println("obj1 instanceof MyInterface: " + (obj1 instanceof MyInterface));
System.out.println("obj2 instanceof Parent: " + (obj2 instanceof Parent));
System.out.println("obj2 instanceof Child: " + (obj2 instanceof Child));
System.out.println("obj2 instanceof MyInterface: " + (obj2 instanceof MyInterface));
}
}
class Parent {}
class Child extends Parent implements MyInterface
{}
interface MyInterface {}"
```

Output:

obj1 instanceof Parent: true
obj1 instanceof Child: false
obj1 instanceof MyInterface: false
obj2 instanceof Parent: true
obj2 instanceof Child: true
obj2 instanceof MyInterface: true

When using the instanceof operator, keep in mind that null is not an instance of anything.

Bitwise and Bit Shift Operators:

The Java programming language also provides operators that perform bitwise and bit shift operations on integral types. The operators discussed in this section are less commonly used. Therefore, their coverage is brief; the intent is to simply make you aware that these operators exist. The following is the list of opertors that come under this category:

~ Unary bitwise complement

<< Signed left shift

>> Signed right shift

>>> Unsigned right shift

& Bitwise AND

^ Bitwise exclusive OR

| Bitwise inclusive OR

The unary bitwise complement operator "~" inverts a bit pattern; it can be applied to any of the integral types, making every "0" a "1" and every "1" a "0". For example, a byte contains 8 bits; applying this operator to a value whose bit pattern is "00000000" would change its pattern to "11111111".

The signed left shift operator "<<" shifts a bit pattern to the left, and the signed right shift operator ">>" shifts a bit pattern to the right. The bit pattern is given by the left-hand operand, and the number of positions to shift by the right-hand operand. The unsigned right shift operator ">>>" shifts a zero into the leftmost position, while the leftmost position after ">>" depends on sign extension.

The bitwise & operator performs a bitwise AND operation.

The bitwise ^ operator performs a bitwise exclusive OR operation.

The bitwise | operator performs a bitwise inclusive OR operation.

The following program, BitDemo, uses the bitwise AND operator to print the number "2" to standard output.

```
"class BitDemo {
  public static void main(String[] args) {
  int bitmask = 0x000F;
  int val = 0x2222;
  // prints "2"
  System.out.println(val & bitmask);
  }}"
```

SECTION II - Applying Object Oriented Concepts in JAVA

Topics Covered in SECTION II:

Classes and Objects in Java

- Object Creation in Java
- Nested and Inner Classes in Java
- More on Classes and Objects in Java

Implementing Inheritance in Java:

- Overriding methods in Jav

Handling Strings in Java:

- Java Program using Strings

V

Classes and Objects in Java

The basic element of object oriented Programming in Java is a class. Class is used to build an Application, to define an applet. A class defines the shape and behavior of an object. In Java, programmers are allowed to define their own classes or can borrow the class definition from outside (such as from built in classes, packages etc)

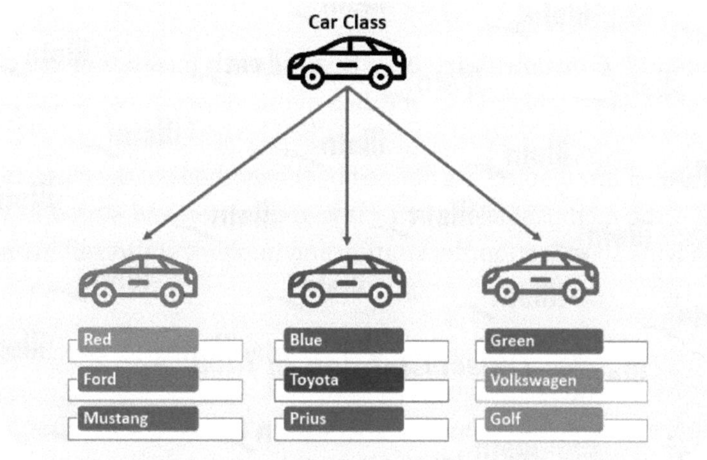

Fig 5.1 Class and Object in Java

A Class is a template for an object. Every object has a class which defines the structure of an object (that means what are various component in it, termed as member elements). The general form of class definition is shown below.

"Class Class Name [extends SuperClassName] [implements Interface] {
[declaration of member elements]
[declaration of methods]
}"

Those are included with [...] are optional. Member elements will be declared with the following syntax :

"type ElementName;"

Methods are declared as follows:

"[Modifier] returnType MethodName (parameter list){
Statements (s) ; // Code for definition of the method.
}"

Putting the member elements and methods into together in the definition of a class called is called encapsulation. Class contains both variables and methods of an object. Variables determine the data to be stored in an object. The code is contained within methods. Collectively, the methods and variables defined within a class are called **members** of the class.

The variables of a class are called **instance variables**, because each instance of the class (i.e., each object of the class) contains its own copy of these variables. Thus, the data of one object are separate and unique from the data of another object.

The operations to be performed by an object are defined by the methods of the class. In Java, both declaration and definition (implementation) of the methods belong to a class are written and stored in the same place and are not separated into two. Because having specification, declaration and implementation all in one place makes for code that is easier to maintain.

Object Creation in Java

Object creation in Java involves two steps:

i. Declare an **object variable** of type class
ii. Create a new object of type class using the **new** keyword and assign its pointer to an object variable.

The first step in object creation is to declare an object variable that will hold the reference to the object to be created. Then create the new object using the class data type and the keyword 'new', which will return the pointer to the newly created object. Assign the object pointer to the object variable declared already in Step 1.

The syntax for declaring and creating an object in Java is as follows:

```
"class class-name
  {
  // members of the class
  }
  class-name obj_variable = new class-name;"
```

An example for the process mentioned above is as follows:

```
class Box
{
double width;
double height;
double depth;
}
Box myBox = new Box( );
```

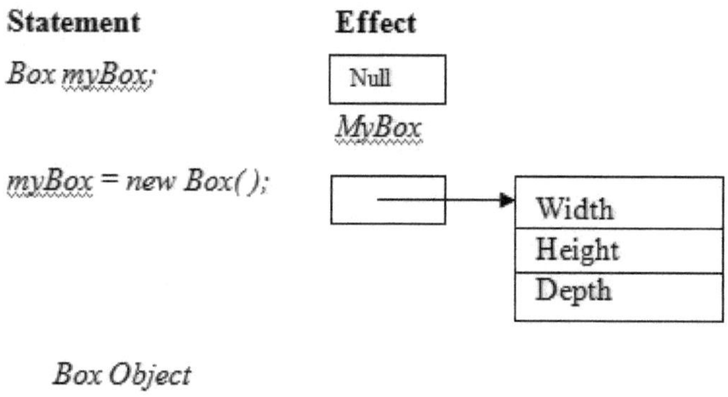

Statement	Effect
Box myBox;	Null *MyBox*
myBox = new Box( );	→ Width / Height / Depth

Box Object

Fig 5.2 - Creating and Using Box Object in Java

In the sample code given above, *Box* is a new data type of type class, which contains three instance variables namely *width, height,* and *depth.* Using this data type *Box*, an object variable *myBox* is declared to hold the reference to an instance of type *Box*. Now the instance variables *width, height,* and *depth* of the newly created object can be accessed using *myBox* and a dot (.) operator:

myBox.width = 100;

Note that the object creation for myBox is done using the single statement:

Box myBox = new Box( );

This statement can be split into the following two lines of code:

```
"Box myBox;
  myBox = new Box( );"
```

In this example, the first line declares a variable of type *Box*, and the second line acquires the actual, physical copy of the object and assigns it to the variable *myBox*. After the execution of second line, we can make use *myBox* as if it were a *Box* object.

But, in reality *myBox* simply holds the memory address of the actual *Box* object. The following figure depicts the process involved in object creation.

Nested and Inner Classes in Java

Nested class is a class defined within another class. The scope of a nested class is bounded by the scope of its enclosing class. For instance, if class A contains a nested class B, the class B is known to A, but not outside of A.

A nested class has access to all the members (which includes private members) of the class in which it is nested. However, the enclosing class doesn't have access to the members of the nested class. Only through the object of the nested class, the enclosing class can access the nested class members. The following program illustrates this:

```
class Outer
{
private int x;
Outer(int a, int b)
{
x = a;
Inner inner = new Inner(b);
}
void Display()
{
```

```
Inner.Display();
}
class Inner
{
int y;
Inner(int a)
{
y = a;
}
void Display()
{
System.out.println("Value of x is : " + x);
System.out.println("Value of y is: " + y);
}
}
}
class InnerDemo
{
public static void main(String args[])
{
Outer outer = new Outer(10, 20);
Outer.Display();
}
}
```

In this sample program, there are three classes defined, namely: *Outer*, *Inner* and *InnerDemo*. *Outer* and *Inner* are classes that define the outer and inner objects respectively. Both classes (*Outer* and *Inner*) have one instance variable (*x*/*y*) and two methods - *Display()* and *a Constructor*.

The object *inner* is instantiated from the constructor of the outer class. While instantiating, the outer class passes an argument to the inner object to set its member variable *y*, i.e., the outer object initializes its inner object through parameter passing.

In the inner class, the member **Display()** has two output statements, one of which accesses the member variable (*x*) of the outer class. This shows the accessibility of the inner class towards the members of its outer class. From the application class *InnerDemo*, we create the object *outer* for which we pass two values 10 and 20 so that both *outer* and *inner* can be initialized with values.

The output of this program will be:

Value of x is: 10
Value of y is: 20

More on Classes and Objects in Java

Objects are created dynamically in Java using the new keyword (operator). In languages like C++, dynamically created objects must be released explicitly by the use of delete operator. But in Java, deletion of objects (i.e., removing the object from memory) is handled automatically. This process of deallocating objects automatically is called Garbage Collection and is done by a program called Garbage Collector.

Garbage Collector is a run-time utility provided in Java for doing garbage collection. It runs behind every Java program and checks periodically for objects that are no longer referenced by any running java program directly or indirectly, and deletes them. When no reference to an object exists, that object is assumed to be no longer needed, and the memory allocated to the object will be reclaimed.

The 'this' keyword:

'**this**' is a keyword that can be used within a method of a class in order to refer to the current instance variables. 'this' must be used to refer to an instance variable, when the same name is given to both - a local variable and a parameter of the method that uses the instance variable. An example is as follows:

```
class Box{
double width;
double height;
double depth;
Box(double width, double height,
double depth){
this.width = width;
this.height = height;
this.depth = depth;
}
}
```

The finalize( ) method:

finalize( ) is a special method, which is similar to destructor in C++. It will run automatically just before an object is destroyed. This method can be used for doing some clean-up operation.

For e.g., if an object is holding some non-java resources such as a file handle or window character font, then such resources must be freed after their usage. This process of freeing the resources before destroying the object that uses them is called finalization.

Argument Passing:

In Java, parameters to a method are passed in two ways: Pass-by-value and Pass-by-reference. In thc first method, a copy of the argument is passed to the subroutine. Therefore, changes made to the parameter of the subroutine have no effect on the argument.

In the second method, a reference to the argument is passed as a parameter. Inside the subroutine, the reference is used to access the actual argument specified in the call. Hence, the changes made to the parameter will affect the argument used to call the subroutine.

Java uses both approaches, depending upon what is passed. When the argument is of primitive data type, it is passed by value. But, if the argument is of type class, it is passed-by-reference. Changes to the object made inside the method do affect the object used as an argument. An example program for passing arguments by reference is as follows:

```
class Data
{
int a, b;
Data(int i, int j)
{
a = i;
b = j;
}
}
class Test
{
void meth(Test o)
{
o.a *= 2;
o.b /= 2;
}
}
class TestAppn
{
```

```
public static void main(String args[])
{
Data D = new Data(15, 20);
System.out.println("Values of a&b before call"+ D.a + ' ` +D.b);
Test T = new Test( );
T.meth(D);
System.out.println("Values of a&b after call" + D.a + ' ` + D.b);
}
}
```

In this example, we have two objects: object D and object T. The first object contains the data or instance variables i and j. Whereas the second object T contains a method meth to do calculations on the data available in the first object. The object D is used as a parameter to the method (meth) of the object T.

The values 15 and 20 are stored in the object D during its creation. Then the method (meth) of the object T is called with the object D passed as an argument. After the call, the method changes the values of object D, which is passed by reference. Therefore the changes made in D by the method of T are made permanent in object D. Then the changed values of object D are displayed using a print statement.

VI
Handling Strings in Java

In Java, a string is a sequence of characters that are stored in an object. Strings are defined and handled by a class named **String**, which is defined in Java's class library.

Every string, be it a constant or variable, is actually an object of type *String*. For e.g., consider the following statement:

System.out.println("this is a string, too");

Here, the string "this is a string, too" is a string constant and also an object.

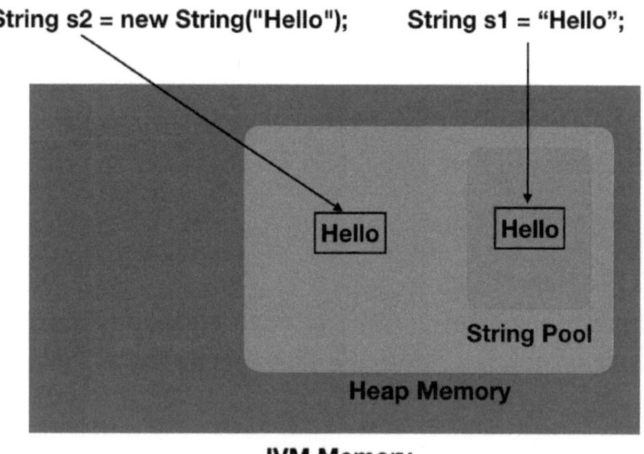

Fig 6.1 - Storing and Managing Strings as Objects in Java

Java provides three classes for handling strings: **String, StringBuffer** and **StringBuilder**. All these classes are declared as final, which means that none of these classes may be sub classed. All these string classes are available in *java.lang* package and hence they are available to all Java programs automatically.

String objects are immutable in java, i.e., once created, they can't be altered, i.e., the content of the string can't be modified. If we want to change a string after its creation, we can do that in any one of the following two ways:

1. Create a new string with modifications.
2. Use the peer class of *String*, called **StringBuffer**, which allows strings to be altered.

Constructing a String:

Strings can be constructed in a variety of ways. The easiest way is to declare a variable of type *String* and assign it with a string as follows:

String myString = "Hello, World!";

After creation, we may use a string object through the program. Two strings can be concatenated (added) to form a new string using the + operator. Following are some examples for creating a new string:

String myString = "I" + " like" + " Java"
String firstname = "Sachin";
String lastname = "Tendulkar";
String name = firstname + lastname;

The *String* class provides several methods for performing operations on strings. Some of the methods are: *equals( ), length( )* and *charAt( )*. The method *equals()* can be used for testing two strings for equality. The function *Length( )* will get you the length of the string. Using *charAt( )*, we can obtain the character at a specified index within a string.

Command-line Arguments:

Command line arguments are information passed as input to a program while starting an application. They are given as strings followed by the program name on the command line to start the application. One or more arguments can be passed to a program from the command line.

To access the command line arguments from a Java application, we have an array of String parameter in the method *main( )*. The following program displays all of the command-line arguments that are passed while running it:

```
class CommandLine {
public static void main(String args[]){
```

```
for (int i = 0; i < args.length; i++)
System.out.println("args[" + i + "]: " + args[i]);
}
}
```

This program can be executed after compilation as follows:

java CommandLine *This is a test for commandline arguments*

The output of this command will be the sequence of strings given after the program name *CommandLine* as shown below:

This is a test for commandline arguments

String Constructors:

The string class supports several constructors, one of which is the default constructor. The default constructor will create an empty string as follows:

String s = new String();

If we want to create a string with initial value, there are varieties of constructors in the *String* class. The general forms of these constructors are as follows:

String(char chars[])

String(char chars[] ,int startIndex, int numChars)

String(String strObj)

String(byte asciiChars[])

String(byte asciiChars[], int startIndex, int numChars)

The **first parameterized constructor** in the above list uses an array of characters to construct the string. All the elements of the character array passed as argument will be used for constructing the string. Example is as follows:

char chars[] = {'a', 'b', 'c'};

String s = new String(chars);

Here, the parameter passed for constructing the string is an array of characters. Hence, the first type of parameterized constructor is called, which initializes the string *s* with the value "abc". If we want to construct the string using a sub range of characters from the character array, then use **the second constructor**:

String(char chars[], int stratIndex, int numChars)

In this constructor, three parameters are used: character Array, starting Index of the array and the No. of characters to be used for constructing the string. An example is as follows:

char chars[] = {'a', 'b', 'c', 'd', 'e', 'f'};

String s = new String(chars, 2, 3);

this initializes s with the string "*cde*".

The third constructor

String(String strObj)

is used for creating a new string from an existing one. The new string will have the same set of characters that of the old one.

The **last two** (constructors) are for creating a string from an array containing ASCII values of set of characters. ASCII values are 8-bit numbers assigned to each and every character in the character sets. The first parameter these constructors is an array of type *byte* that contains the ASCII codes of the characters to use in constructing the string. An example is as follows:

byte ascii[] = {65,66,67,68,69,70};

String s1 = new String(ascii);

These two lines of code will initialize the string s1 with *abcdef.*

String Literal:

String literal is nothing but a string placed within double quotes. For instance, "abc" is a string literal. For each and every string literal in the program, Java automatically constructors a string object. Thus we can use a string literal to initialize a string object as follows:

String s1 = "abc";

String Concatenation:

String concatenation is nothing but combing two strings into one. It can be done in two ways: using + operator or using *concat( )* method. Concatenation using the first method is similar to Add operation. The second method uses the method of String object for concatenation.

While concatenation, when two strings used as operands, they will be simply joined together. When one of the operands is of different type, it will be converted first before used in concatenation. For e.g.,

String s = "four:" + 2 + 2;

will initialize the string s with the string "four: 22" rather than "four: 4".

Java Program using Strings

Here is the algorithm and a program written in Java to get a name (string of characters) from the user and to find out the following:

- Length of the name

- Character 'a' is present or not in the name
- Location of 'a' present in the name

Algirithm:

1. Declare an object of String named sName
2. Declare variables of type int namely lCount, nIndex and fIndex for finding the length of the name, next index of 'a' and first index for searching the next occurance of 'a' in sName
3. Get the name from the user and store it in sName using the object din of type DataInputStream
4. Call the method length() of string object sName for finding the length and store it in lCount
5. Call the method indexOf() of sName to find 'a' exists in it or not and store its result in nIndex
6. Repeat the following until nIndex > 0 (i.e., next occurrence of 'a' exist)
7. Print nIndex
8. Set fIndex with the next value of nIndex (nIndex + 1)
9. Call indexOf() on sName with the help of fIndex

Program:

```
import java.util.Scanner;
    public class StringObj
    {
    public static void main(String[] args)
    {
    String sName;
    int lCount, nIndex=0, fIndex;
    Scanner scan = new Scanner(System.in);
    System.out.print("Enter a String: ");
    sName = scan.nextLine();
    System.out.println("The given String is : " + sName);
    lCount = sName.length();
    System.out.println("The length of the given String is : " + lCount);
```

```
nIndex = sName.indexOf('a');
if (nIndex > 0)
{
System.out.println("The letter 'a' is Present in the given String");
System.out.println("The letter 'a' appears in the following Indexes :");
while (nIndex > 0)
{
System.out.println(nIndex + " ");
fIndex = nIndex + 1;
nIndex = sName.indexOf('a',fIndex);
}
}
}
}
```

Sample Run:

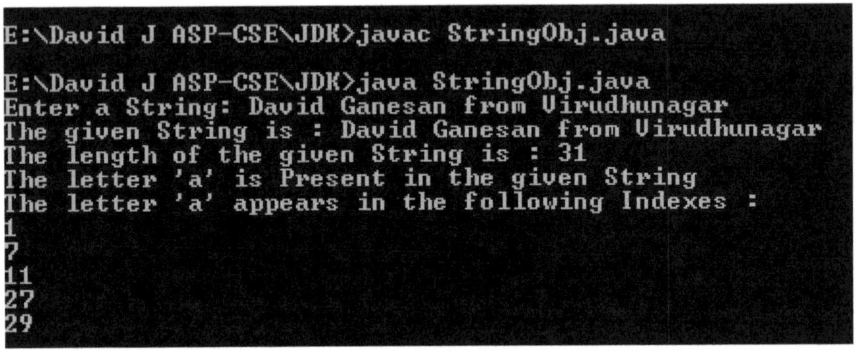

```
E:\David J ASP-CSE\JDK>javac StringObj.java

E:\David J ASP-CSE\JDK>java StringObj.java
Enter a String: David Ganesan from Virudhunagar
The given String is : David Ganesan from Virudhunagar
The length of the given String is : 31
The letter 'a' is Present in the given String
The letter 'a' appears in the following Indexes :
1
7
11
27
29
```

Fig 6.2 - Sample Input and Output of a Program that uses String Object

VII

Implementing Inheritance in JAVA

Using the concept inheritance in Java, we can create a general class that defines traits common to a set of related objects. This class can then be inherited by other, more specific classes, each adding those things that are unique to it.

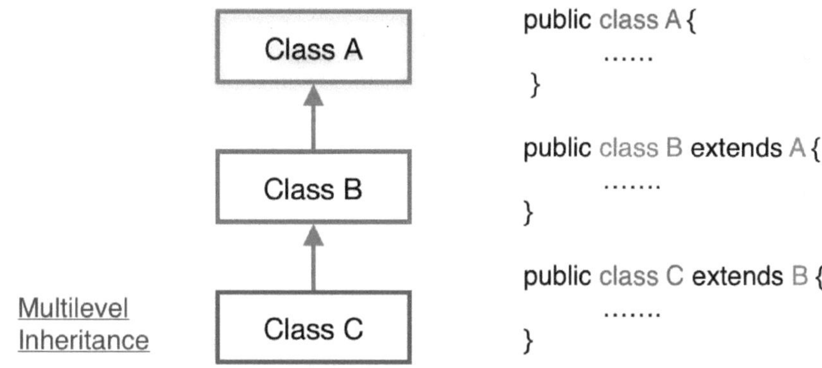

Fig 7.1 Multilevel Inheritance in Java

In Java, a class that is inherited is called a **super class**. The class that does the inheritance is called a **sub class**. A sub class is a specialized version of a super class. It inherits all of the instance variables and methods defined by the super class and add its own, unique elements.

The 'extends' keyword:

Inheritance can be implemented in Java using the 'extends' keyword. Use the keyword **extends** next to the class name of the sub class, followed by the base class name. The general form of the class that inherits a super class is shown here:

```
"class subclass_name extends superclass_name
  {
  // body of the class
  }"
```

During inheritance a sub class can be directly inherited from only one super class, i.e., we can only specify one super class for any sub class that extends. Java doesn't support the inheritance of multiple super classes for creating a sub class. Instead, it allows **multilevel inheritance**, in which a sub class becomes a super class of another sub class.

Although a sub class includes all of the members of its super class, it can't access the private members of the super class. Therefore, a reference variable of a super class can be assigned a reference to any of its sub class. But, a reference variable of a sub class can't hold a reference to a super class object.

The Following is an example program for inheritance in Java:

```
class Box{
double width;
double height;
double depth;
Box(double w, double h, double d){
width = w;
height = h;
depth = d;
}
double Volume( ){
return width * height * depth;
}
}
class ColorBox extends Box
{
int color;
```

```
ColorBox(double w, double h, double d, int c){
width = w;
height = h;
depth = d;
color = c;
}
}
```

In this example, we have two classes: **Box** and **ColorBox**. Box is a super class and the ColorBox is a sub class. Box provides three instance variables (*width, height* and *depth*) and two methods (a constructor and *volume*). The *ColorBox* is a type of *Box* which adds another instance variable *color*.

After inheritance, the new class *ColorBox* contains four instance variables (*width, height, depth and color*) and three methods (two constructors and the method *volume*). As all the members of the super class are public by default, they are inherited and accessed freely by the sub class *ColorBox*.

Accessing the Base Class members from Subclass:

When the instance variables of the super class are private in scope, they can't be directly accessed from a sub class. The private members of the super class can be accessed from a sub class only through the methods of the base class. But, the public members of the super class can be called by name from the sub class, except for constructors.

To call the constructor of the super class use the method ***super( )***. When a sub class object is created, super class' default constructor will be called automatically unless it is called explicitly from the sub class' constructor.

Given a sub class B and a super class A, constructors are called in the order of derivation, from super class to sub class. Hence, *super( )* must be the first statement to be executed in a sub class' constructor, whether explicitly specified or not.

The following example illustrates this:

```
class Box
{
private double width;
private double height;
private double depth;
Box(double w, double h, double d)
{
width = w;
height = h;
depth = d;
```

```
}
double Volume( )
{
return width * height * depth;
}
}
class ColorBox extends Box
{
int color;
ColorBox(double w, double h, double d, int c)
{
super(w, h, d);
color = c;
}
}
class BoxAppn
{
public static void main(String args[])
{
Box mybox1 = new Box(10, 20, 15);
Box mybox2 = new ColorBox(3, 6, 9, 1001);
double vol;
vol = box1.volume();
System.out.println("The volume of box1 is : " + vol);
vol = box2.volume();
System.out.println("The volume of box1 is : " + vol);
}
}
```

In this program, the instance variables of the base class (*width, height* and *depth*) are declared in the private scope. Hence, these variables are inherited by the sub class *ColoBox* without having any access permission on them. The only way to access the private members of the super class from a sub class is through the methods of the super class.

Now, to assign the initial values to the private members of the super class from the sub class, we call the super class constructor using the method *super( )* as in the above example. The newly added variable *color* can be accessed directly from the methods of *BoxAppn* (sub class).

Multilevel Inheritance in Java

In multi-level inheritance, classes are arranged in many levels. The parent classes are in the top level, from which child (sub) classes are derived. Similarly, child classes are further used for deriving another set of classes called grand-children. The following Java code demonstrates the implementation of Multi-level Inheritance in Java:

```
class A
{
A()
{
System.out.println("A's constructor called");
}
}
class B extends A {
B(){
System.out.println("B's constructor called");
}
}
class C extends B {
C() {
System.out.println("C's constructor called");
}
}
class TestAppn {
public static void main(String args[]) {
C cObj = new C();
}
}
```

In this example, the following will be the output when the object *cObj* is created from the method main() of *TestAppn*:

A's constructor called
B's constructor called
C's constructor called

Because, as soon as the new object *cObj* is created, the default constructor of the new object will be called automatically. As the newly created object is an object of the derived class, before executing the derived class constructor all its super class constructors will be called first, in the order of their derivation.

Overriding Methods in JAVA

In a class hierarchy, when a method in a sub class has the same name and type signature of a method in its super class, the method in the sub class is said to over ride the method in the super class.

The version of the method defined by the super class will be hidden in the sub class by its overriding method. When an overridden method is called through the object of the sub class, the version of the method defined by the sub class will be invoked for execution.

The 'super' keyword:

'*super*' is a keyword used from a sub class to access the members of the super class. It can be also be used for the following purposes:

1. To access an over ridden member of a super class from its sub class.
2. To access a hidden instance variable of a super class from its sub class.

To call the overridden method of a super class use the keyword ***super*** followed by dot (.) and the method name. But to call the overridden constructor simply use the keyword followed by parenthesis with zero or more parameters:

super( )

To access the hidden instance variable of the super class, use the keyword super followed by (.) and the instance variable name. The following example is an illustration for the use of keyword *super*:

```
class A {
int i;
A(int a) {
i = a;
}
void Show() {
System.out.println("The value of I is " + I);
}
}
class B extends A {
int i;
B(int a, int b) {
super.i = a;
```

```
i = b;
}
void Show() {
super.Show();
System.out.println("The value of i in the Sub class is " + i);
}
}
class TestAppn {
public static void main(Strings args[]) {
A ptrA = new B(10, 20);
ptrA.Show();
}
}
```

In this example, we have two classes, both containing the variable *i* and the method *Show( )*. To access the base class (A) members *i* and *Show( )* from the sub class B, we need to use the keyword *super* as discussed above. Because, the instance variable *i* of the super class is hidden in the sub class and the method *Show( )* is overridden in the sub class.

The third class in the above java program is the application class. It contains the method *main( )*, the starting point of any java application. In main( ), a new object of type B is created and assigned to a pointer of type A, i.e., the subclass object is created and assigned to the pointer of super class. Then the method *Show( )* of the newly created object is called. This will invoke the method *Show( )* of the sub class, because the pointer points the object of the sub class, from which the super class *Show( )* is called through the keyword *super*.

Use of 'final' keyword in inheritance:

A method declared as **final** in the super class can't be overridden in its sub classes. To declare methods as a final one use the keyword *final* as prefix to its header. The keyword **final** can also be used for declaring a class as a final one. Declaring a class as final implicitly declares all of its methods as final, too. A final class can't be used for inheritance.

Abstract Class:

Abstract class is a super class in Java with one or more abstract methods in it. An abstract class defines a generalized form or the structure of a kind of object that will be shared by all of its sub classes. The abstract methods of an abstract class will have only the function header but not the body. The body of the function will be provided in the sub class derived from such a super class.

To declare a super class as an abstract one, use the keyword **abstract** in front of the class keyword at the beginning of the class declaration. To declare methods as **abstract methods** use the keyword *abstract* as prefix in the method signature. The general form of the abstract method is:

abstract type name(parameter list);

An abstract class can't be used for object creation. Instead it must be inherited into a subclass with the implementations for all the abstract methods and then the objects created of that sub type.

VIII
Handling Input and Output using Streams

In Java, input to a program may come from the keyboard, the mouse, the memory, the disk, a network or another program. Similarly, output from a program may go to the screen, the printer, the memory, the disk, a network or another program. Although the input and output devices look very different at the hardware level, they share certain common characteristics such as:

1. Unidirectional movement of data
2. Treating data as a sequence of bytes or characters and
3. Support of sequential access to the data

Hence, Java uses the concept of streams to represent the ordered sequence of data, a common characteristic shared by all I/O devices. A stream presents a uniform, easy-to-use, object-oriented interface between the program and I/O devices.

A stream in Java is a path along which data flows. It has a source and a destination. The source and the destination may refer to physical devices or programs or other streams in the same program. Java streams are classified into two basic types namely Input stream and Output stream.

An **input stream** extracts (i.e. reads) data from the source and send them to the program. Similarly, an output stream takes data from the program and sends (i.e. writes) them to the destination. In both cases, the program doesn't know the details of end points (i.e., source and destination).

Stream Classes

To support stream oriented I/O, Java provides **java.io** package, which contains a large number of stream classes that provide capabilities for all types of I/O. These classes may be grouped into two groups based on the data type on which they operate:

1. Byte stream classes that provide support for handling I/O on bytes and
2. Character stream classes that provide support for managing I/O on characters

These two groups may be further classified based on their purpose. Byte stream classes have been designed to provide functional features for reading and writing bytes of data from streams and files; whereas character stream classes are designed to read and write 16-bit Unicode characters.

Byte Streams:

The package java.io provides two set of class hierarchies - one for handling reading and writing of bytes, and another for handling reading and writing of characters. The abstract classes InputStream and OutputStream are the root of inheritance hierarchies handling reading and writing of bytes respectively.

The java.io package contains several subclasses of InputStream and OutputStream that implement specific input/ output functions. For example, FileInputStream and FileOutputStream are input and output stream classes that operate on files on the native file system. Similarly Reader and Writer classes are streams that operate on character input and output respectively.

Three Objects for I/O:

Three objects are provided in the System object for handling the input, output and error in Java. They are named as **in**, **out** and **err** and are of type static. The object 'in' is of **InputStream** type and the other two are of **PrintStream** type. With the help of these objects, we can get the input from the user through keyboard, send the output to the screen, and display error messages if any error occurs. The root object – **System** is available in the package java.lang, and is accessible by default from every Java program.

Storing the Input Data:

Data to be stored in a variable can be obtained through the keyboard using the *readLine()* method of the DataInputStream object. The *readLine()* method reads the input from the keyboard as a string that can be converted to another data type using the wrapper class provided for the corresponding data type.

Java provides five primitive data types for data storage, namely int, float, long, char and double. It also provides wrapper classes in its java.lang package for converting primitive data types into object data type. The wrapper classes help the user store their data in objects. Such classes are listed below:

Primitive Datatype	Wrapper Classes
Boolean	Boolean
Char	Character
Double	Double
Float	Float
Int	Integer
Long	Long

Fig 8.1 Wrapper Classes Equivalent of Primitive Data Types

The following Java program illustrates the use of Wrapper Classes for converting scalar data into an object:

```
class Reading {
public static void main(String args[]){
DataInputStream in = new DataInputStream(System.in);
int intNo = 0;
float floatNo = 0.0f;
try
{
System.out.println("Enter an Integer:");
intNo = Integer.parseInt(in.readLine());
System.out.println("Enter a float No.");
floatNo = Float.valueOf(in.readLine()).floatValue();
}
catch(Exception e)
{}
System.out.println("intNumber = " + intNo);
System.out.println("floatNumber = " + floatNo);
}
```

}

In the above java program, user input is obtained twice with the help of the readLine() method of the input (in) object. The given input is in the form of string of characters, which is then converted into integer and float using the wrapper classes Integer and Float respectively. The method parseInt() of Integer class converts the string data into an integer value. Similarly, the valueOf() method of the Float class converts the input data into a floating value. The method floatValue() of the Float class retrieves the floating point value in a floating-point notation.

Input Stream Classes:

Input stream classes are byte stream classes that are used to read 8 bit byte data. All the input stream classes are arranged in a hierarchy structure. InputStream class is the root class in the hierarchy. This class is an abstract class, which can't be used for object creation. It provides the basic functionalities for performing the following operations on input: Reading bytes, Closing streams, Marking positions in streams, Skipping ahead in streams and Finding the number of bytes in a stream data.

The following figure shows the class hierarchy of input stream classes:

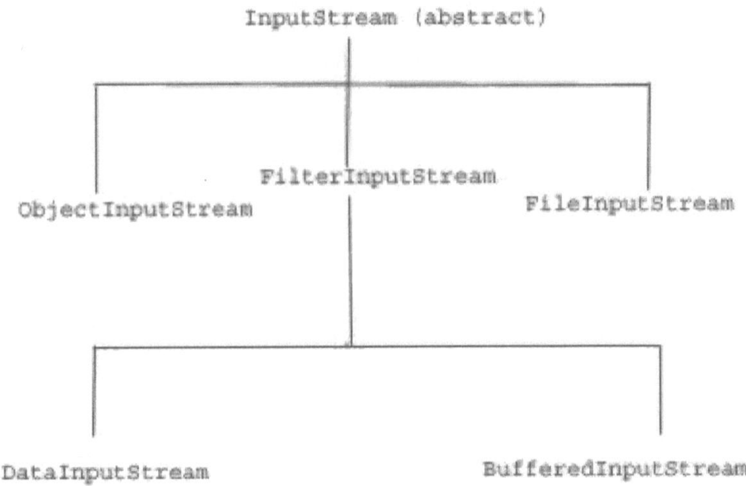

Fig 8.2 InputStream Class Hierarchy (Partial)

InputStream class defines the following methods for reading bytes

"*int read() throws IOException*
int read(byte b[]) throws IOException
int read(byte b[], int offset, int length) throws IOException"

Subclasses of InputStream implement the above mentioned methods. Other methods defined in InputStream are: available(), skip(), reset() & close().

The class DataInputStream is a sub class that extends FilterInputStream and implements the interface DataInput. Therefore, the DataInputStream class implements the methods described in DataInput in addition to the methods inherite3d from InputStream class. The DataInput interface contains the following method:

- readShort()
- readLine()
- reading()
- readChar()
- readLong()
- readBoolean()
- readFloat()
- readDouble()

The example below illustrates code to read a character.

"*//First create an object of type FileInputStream type using the name of the file.*
FileInputStream inp = new FileInputStream("filename.ext");
//Create an object of type DataInputStream using inp.
DataInputStream dataInp = new DataInputStream(inp);
int i = dataInp.readInt();"

Jazmin

Output Stream Classes:

The OutputStream class is the base class of all output streams in the Java IO API. Subclasses include the BufferedOutputStream and the FileOutputStream among others. OutputStream's are used for writing byte based data, one byte at a time. Here is an example: The write() method of an OutputStream takes an int which contains the byte value of the byte to write.

Subclasses of OutputStream may have alternative write() methods. For instance, the DataOutputStream allows you to write Java primitives like int, long, float, double, boolean etc. with its corresponding methods writeBoolean(), writeDouble() etc. The following figure shows the class hierarchy of OutputStream classes:

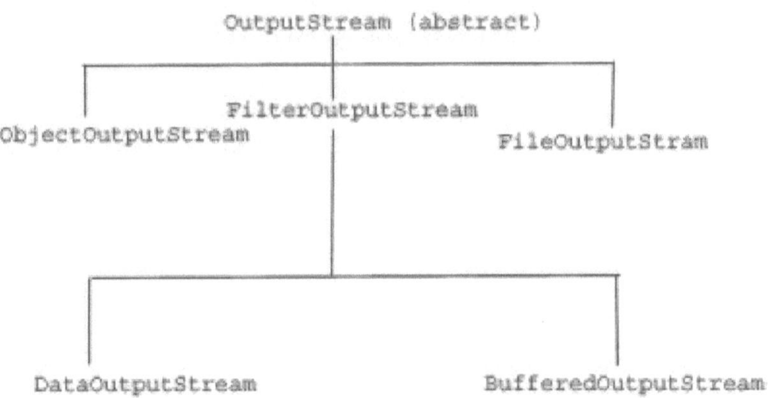

Fig 8.3 OutputStream Class Hierarchy (Partial)

OutputStream class defines the following methods for writing bytes –

"*void write(int b) throws IOException*
void write(byte b[]) throws IOException
void write(byte b[], int offset, int length) throws IOException"

Subclasses of OutputStream implement the above mentioned methods.

IX
Exception Handling in Java

An exception is an abnormal condition that many arise from a code sequence at run time. Exception handling is a mechanism provided in programming languages like C++ and Java for handling the exception that may arise during the execution of a program. In other words, an exception is a run-time error.

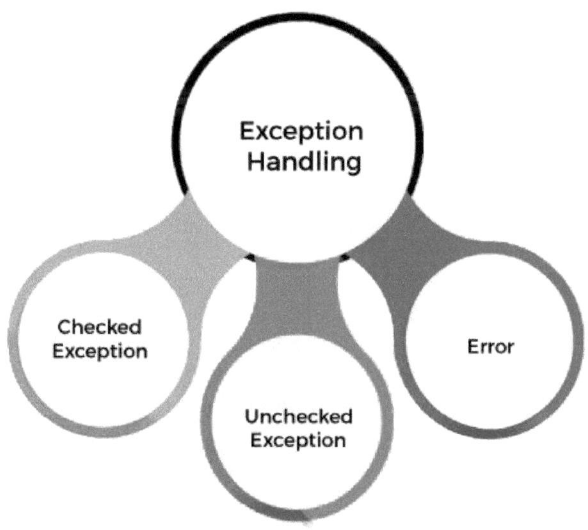

Fig 9.1 - Three basic Classiciations of Exceptions in Java

In computer languages that do not support exception handling, errors must be checked and handled manually – typically through the use of error codes.

How Exceptions are handled in Java?

In Java, exceptions are handled using objects of type Exception. An exception in Java is an object that describes the exceptional (i.e. error) condition that may arise from a piece of code. When an exceptional condition occurs, an object representing that exception is created and thrown from the method that caused the error. Thrown exceptions are caught by a special piece of code, called catch block, in order to take remedial action for the particular error condition.

Generally, exceptions are raised from the code that violates the rules of the language or the constraints of the run-time environment of the language. Exceptions are raised implicitly by Java run-time system or explicitly (manually) by a piece of code. Manually generated exceptions are typically used to report some error condition to the caller of a method.

Exception Types:

Exceptions that can be handled in Java are defined in a hierarchy of classes, called Exception classes. All exception classes are subclasses of the built-in class Throwable. Thus, Throwable is at the top of the exception class hierarchy. Immediately below Throwable are two sub classes namely Exception and Error. These two classes define the two major classifications of exception. The class Exception defines all exceptions that can be handled by the user from the code; whereas, the Error class defines the exceptions that are not expected to be caught under normal circumstances.

Exceptions of type Error are used by Java run-time system to indicate the errors that can be handled only by run-time environment. Stack overflow is an exception of type Error. There is an important subclass of Exception, called RunTimeException, which is used for handling exceptions that include division by zero and invalid array indexing.

Five Keywords:

Java exception handling mechanism provides five keywords for handling exceptions, namely try, catch, throw, throws and finally. The keyword try is used for defining a block of code that contains one or more statements, which will be monitored by the run-time system for exceptions. If an exception occurs during the execution of a try block, such exceptions are thrown to the catch block by run-time system.

System generated exceptions are automatically thrown by the Java run-time system. To manually throw an exception, use the keyword throw. Thrown exceptions are handled in a Java program using a block of code called catch block.

Any exception that is thrown out of a method must be specified in the header part of the method using throws clause. Any code that must be executed before a method returns is put in a finally block. The general form of an exception handling block is shown below:

```
"try{
  //block of code to be monitored for errors
  }
  catch(ExceptionType1 exob) {
  // exception handler for ExceptionType1
  }
  catch(ExceptionType2 exob) {
  // exception handler for ExpcetionType2
  }
  finally{
  // block of code to be executed before try block ends
  }"
```

Here, the ExpceptionType is the type of the exception that has occurred. Any exception that is not caught by the program will ultimately be processed by the default handler. The default exception handler displays a string describing the exception, prints a stack trace from the point at which the exception occurred, and the program terminates. In order to avoid such abrupt termination of a Java program, we need to handle the exception properly.

Using try and catch Blocks:

To guard a block of code against run-time error during its execution, simply enclose that code inside the try block. Next to the try block, include a catch block along with a parameter that specifies the exception type of the exception to be handled. The following program illustrates the use of try block along with a catch block which process the exception named ArithmeticException generated due to division-by-zero error:

```
class ExceptHandle{
public static void main(String args[])
{
int d, a;
try{ // monitor a block of code
d = 0;
a = 42 / d;
```

```
System.out.println("This will not be printed...");
}
catch(ArithmeticException e) {
System.out.println("Divison by Zero occurred...");
}
System.out.println("Exception resumes here...");
}
}
```

This program will generate the following output:

"Division by Zero occurred...
Execution resumes here...
In the above example, the statement
a = 42 / d;"

results in a division-by-zero error, which throws the exception ArithmeticException to Java run-time system. In response, Java run-time system will transfer the program control from the try block to the catch block, which has the object of type ArithmeticException as its parameter. After the execution of catch block, the program control will be transferred to the next statement that follows the entire try/catch block. That means, the control will never return back to the try block for the execution of remaining statements in the try block. That is why the above program prints two lines of output.

A try and its corresponding catch block form a unit. In some cases, more than one exception could be raised by a single try block. To handle such situation, we need to define two or more catch blocks, each catching a different type of exception. All the catch blocks that follow a single try block are considered as a single unit. And each catch block is associated with only one try block, which immediately precedes the catch block(s).

When an exception is thrown, each catch block is inspected in order, and the first exception whose type matches the type of the exception being thrown is selected for execution. After its execution, the program control transfers to the next statement that follows the entire try/catch block, bypassing all the remaining catch blocks associated with the try block.

Displaying the Error Message:

Every exception is an object of type String, which contains the description of the exception that occurred. We can display the description of the exception being raised by passing the exception object as an argument to the println method. The following piece of code illustrates this:

```
catch(ArithmeticException e) {
System.out.println("Exception: " + e);
a = 0;
}
```

When an exception of type ArithmeticException is thrown, the above catch block will display the following error message:

Exception: java.lang.ArithmeticException; /by zero

The 'finally' block:

The keyword 'finally' is used to create a block of code that will be executed after the execution of a try/catch block and before proceeding further for executing the code that follows the try/catch block. This block of code will be executed whether or not an exception occurs from within the try block. If an exception occurs, the finally block will be executed after handling the exception. This block will be executed even if there is no exception handler (catch block) provided for the exception being raised.

The finally block is optional. However, each try statement requires at least one catch or a finally block for handling the error. This block of code is useful for closing file handles and freeing up any other resources that might have been allocated at the beginning of a method of a method with the intent of disposing them before its return.

SECTION III - Developing Java Applications

Experiment 1:

Develop a Java application to generate Electricitybill. Create a class with the following members: Consumer no., consumer name, previous month reading, current month reading, type of EB connection(i.e domestic or commercial).

Compute the bill amount using the following tariff.If the type of the EB connection is domestic, calculate the amount to be paid as follows:

- First 100 units -Rs. 1 per unit
- 101-200 units -Rs. 2.50 per unit
- 201 -500 units -Rs. 4 per unit
- > 501 units -Rs. 6 per unit

If the type of the EB connection is commercial, calculate the amount to be paid as follows:

- First 100 units -Rs. 2 per unit
- 101-200 units -Rs. 4.50 per unit
- 201 -500 units -Rs. 6 per unit
- > 501 units -Rs. 7 per unit

Experiment 2:

Develop a java application to implement currency converter (Dollar to INR, EURO to INR, Yen to INR and vice versa), distance converter (meter to KM, miles to KM and vice versa) , time converter (hours to minutes, seconds and vice versa) using packages.

Experiment 3:

Develop a java application with Employee class with Emp_name, Emp_id, Address, Mail_id, Mobile_no as members. Inherit the classes, Programmer, Assistant Professor, Associate Professor and Professor from employee class. Add Basic Pay (BP) as the member of all the inherited classes with 97% of BP as DA, 10 % of BP as HRA, 12% of BP as PF, 0.1% of BPfor staff club fund. Generatepay slipsfor the employees with their gross and net salary.

Experiment 4:

Design a Java interface for ADT Stack. Implement this interface using array. Provide necessary exception handling in both the implementations.

Experiment 5:

Write a program to perform string operations using ArrayList. Write functions for the followinga. Append -add at endb. Insert –add at particular indexc. Searchd. List all string starts with given letter

Experiment 6:

Write a Java Program to create an abstract class named Shape that contains two integers and an empty method named print Area(). Provide three classes named Rectangle, Triangle and Circle such that each one of the classes extends the class Shape. Each one of the classes contains only the method print Area () that prints the area of the given shape.

Experiment 7:

Write a Java program to implement user defined exception handling.

Experiment 8:

Write a Java program that readsa file name from the user,displays information about whether the file exists, whether the file is readable, or writable, the type of file and the length of the file in bytes.

Experiment 9:

Write a java program that implements a multi-threadedapplication that has three threads. First thread generates a random integer every 1 second and if the value is even, second thread computes the square of the number and prints. If the value is odd, the third thread will print the value of cube of the number.

Experiment 10:

Write a java program to find the maximum value from the given type of elements using a generic function.

Experiment 11:

Design a calculator using event-driven programming paradigm of Java with the following options. a) Decimal manipulationsb) Scientific manipulations

Experiment 12:

Develop a mini project for any application using Java concepts.

X

Experiments 1 & 2 of OOP Lab (CS8383)

EXERCISE 1

Develop a Java application to generate Electricity bill. Create a class with the following members: Consumer no., consumer name, previous month reading, current month reading, type of EB connection (i.e domestic or commercial).

Compute the bill amount using the following tariff:
If the type of the EB connection is domestic, calculate the amount to be paid as follows:
1. First 100 units - Rs. 1 per unit
2. 101-200 units - Rs. 2.50 per unit
3. 201 -500 units - Rs. 4 per unit
4. > 501 units - Rs. 6 per unit

If the type of the EB connection is commercial, calculate the amount to be paid as follows:
1. First 100 units - Rs. 2 per unit
2. 101-200 units - Rs. 4.50 per unit
3. 201 -500 units - Rs. 6 per unit
4. > 501 units - Rs. 7 per unit

PROGRAM:

```
    import java.util.*;
    class EBCalculator{
Scanner in = new Scanner(System.in);
Scanner ins = new Scanner(System.in);
    String cname, type;
int bn;
double current, previous, tbill, units;
    void getData()
{
System.out.print ("\n\t Enter consumer number ");
bn = in.nextInt();
    System.out.print ("\n\t Enter Type of connection (D for Domestic or C for Commercial) ");
type = ins.nextLine();
    System.out.print ("\n\t Enter consumer name ");
cname = ins.nextLine();
    System.out.print ("\n\t Enter previous month reading ");
previous= in.nextDouble();
    System.out.print ("\n\t Enter current month reading ");
current= in.nextDouble();
}
    void calcBillAmt()
{
units = current - previous;
    if(type.equals("D"))
{
if (units<=100) tbill=1 * units;
else if (units>100 && units<=200) tbill=2.50*units;
else if(units>200 && units<=500) tbill= 4*units;
else tbill= 6*units;
}
else
{
if (units<=100) tbill= 2 * units;
else if(units>100 && units<=200) tbill=4.50*units;
else if(units>200 && units<=500) tbill= 6*units;
```

```
else tbill= 7*units;
}
}
    void displayBill()
{
System.out.println("\n\t Consumer number = "+bn);
System.out.println ("\n\t Consumer name = "+cname);
if(type.equals("D"))
System.out.println ("\n\t type of connection = DOMESTIC ");
else
System.out.println ("\n\t type of connection = COMMERCIAL ");
    System.out.println ("\n\t Current Month Reading = "+current);
System.out.println ("\n\t Previous Month Reading = "+previous);
System.out.println ("\n\t Total units = "+units);
System.out.println ("\n\t Total bill = RS "+tbill);
}
}
    class Main{
public static void main (String args[])
{
EBCalculator ebc = new EBCalculator();
ebc.getData();
ebc.calcBillAmt();
ebc.displayBill();
}}
```

SAMPLE INPUT & OUTPUT:

```
Enter consumer number 74384738

Enter Type of connection (D for Domestic or C for Commercial) D

Enter consumer name David Livingston J

Enter previous month reading 780

Enter current month reading 900
```

Fig 10.1 Sample Input for EBCalculator

```
Consumer number = 74384738

Consumer name = David Livingston J

type of connection = DOMESTIC

Current Month Reading = 900.0

Previous Month Reading = 780.0

Total units = 120.0

Total bill = RS 300.0
```

Fig 10.2 Sample Output of EBCalculator

EXERCISE 2

Develop a java application to implement currency converter (Dollar to INR, EURO to INR, Yen to INR and vice versa), distance converter (meter to KM, miles to KM and vice versa) using packages.

ConvertDemo.java

```
import java.util.*;
import Converter.CurrencyConvert;
import Converter.DistanceConvert;
public class ConverterDemo
{
public static void main(String args[])
{
int choice;
double amt;
Scanner sc = new Scanner(System.in);

System.out.println("hi, Welcome to the Currency Converter!");
System.out.println("which currency You want to Convert ? ");
System.out.println("1:Ruppe \t2:Dollar \n3:Euro \t4:Yen ");
choice = sc.nextInt();

System.out.println("How much Money you want to convert ?");
amt = sc.nextFloat();

CurrencyConvert c1;
c1 = new CurrencyConvert(choice, amt);
c1.convert();

System.out.println("\nhi, Welcome to the Distance Converter!");
DistanceConvert d1;
d1 = new DistanceConvert();
d1.convert();
}
}
```

CurrencyConvert.java

```
package Converter;
import java.util.*;
import java.text.DecimalFormat;

public class CurrencyConvert
{
int code;
double amount, dollar, euro, yen, rupee;
DecimalFormat f = new DecimalFormat("##.##");
Scanner sc = new Scanner(System.in);
public CurrencyConvert(int c, double a)
{
code = c;
amount = a;
}

public void convert()
{

// For amounts Conversion
switch (code) {
//For Rupee Conversion
case 1:
dollar = amount / 70;
System.out.println("Your " + amount + " Rupee is : " + f.format(dollar) + " Dollar");

euro = amount / 80;
System.out.println("Your " + amount + " Rupee is : " + f.format(euro) + " Euro");

yen = amount / 0.63;
System.out.println("Your " + amount + " Rupee is : " + f.format(yen) + " Yen");
break;

// For Dollar Conversion
case 2:
```

```
rupee = amount * 70;
System.out.println("Your " + amount + " Dollar is : " + f.format(rupee) + " Ruppes");

euro = amount * 0.87;
System.out.println("Your " + amount + " Dollar is : " + f.format(euro) + " Euro");

yen = amount * 111.087;
System.out.println("Your " + amount + " Dollar is : " + f.format(yen) + " Yen");
break;

// For Euro Conversion
case 3:
rupee = amount * 80;
System.out.println("Your " + amount + " euro is : " + f.format(rupee) + " Ruppes");

dollar = amount * 1.14;
System.out.println("Your " + amount + " euro is : " + f.format(dollar) + " Dollar");

yen = amount * 127.32;
System.out.println("Your " + amount + " euro is : " + f.format(yen) + " Yen");
break;

// For Yen Conversion
case 4:
rupee = amount * 0.63;
System.out.println("Your " + amount + " yen is : " + f.format(rupee) + " Ruppes");

dollar = amount * 0.008;
System.out.println("Your " + amount + " yen is : " + f.format(dollar) + " Dollar");

euro = amount * 0.007;
System.out.println("Your " + amount + " yen is : " + f.format(euro) + " Euro");
break;

default:
```

```
System.out.println("Invalid input");
}
}
}
```

DistanceConvert.java

```
package Converter;
import java.util.*;
public class DistanceConvert
{
static double convertIntoKms(double miles){
double km=1.609*miles;
return km;
}


static double convertIntoMiles(double km){
double miles=km/1.609;
return miles;
}

static double convertMeterIntoKms(double meter){
double km=meter/1000;
return km;
}

static double convertKmsIntoMeter(double km){
double meter = km * 1000;
return meter;
}
public void convert()
{
try{
Scanner sc = new Scanner(System.in);
System.out.print("Enter Distance in Miles : ");
double miles = sc.nextDouble();
```

```
System.out.println(miles+" Miles equal to : "+convertIntoKms(miles)+" KMs");

System.out.print("Enter Distance in Km : ");
double kms = sc.nextDouble();
System.out.println(kms+" KMs equal to : "+convertIntoMiles(kms)+" Miles");

//Meter to KM and KM to Meter conversion
System.out.print("Enter Distance in Meter : ");
double meter = sc.nextDouble();
System.out.println(meter + " Meter is equal to : " + convertMeterIntoKms(meter) + " KMs");

System.out.print("Enter Distance in Km : ");
kms = sc.nextDouble();
System.out.println(kms + " KMs equal to : " + convertKmsIntoMeter(kms)+" Meters");
}
catch(Exception E){
System.err.println("Exception : "+E.getMessage());
}
}
}
```

SAMPLE INPUT & OUTPUT:

```
Command Prompt
C:\CSE\Java>javac ConverterDemo.java

C:\CSE\Java>java ConverterDemo
hi, Welcome to the Currency Converter!
which currency You want to Convert ?
1:Ruppe         2:Dollar
3:Euro  4:Yen
1
How much Money you want to convert ?
3000
Your 3000.0 Rupee is : 42.86 Dollar
Your 3000.0 Rupee is : 37.5 Euro
Your 3000.0 Rupee is : 4761.9 Yen

hi, Welcome to the Distance Converter!
Enter Distance in Miles  : 15
15.0 Miles equal to : 24.134999999999998 KMs
Enter Distance in Km  : 20
20.0 KMs equal to : 12.430080795525171 Miles
Enter Distance in Meter  : 2000
2000.0 Meter is equal to : 2.0 KMs
Enter Distance in Km  : 20
20.0 KMs equal to : 20000.0 Meters

C:\CSE\Java>
```

Fig 10.3 Sample Input and Output of Converter (Currency & Distance) in Java

9 798885 307529

Printed by Libri Plureos GmbH in Hamburg,
Germany